THE
ASTROLOGY
PUZZLE
BOOK

About the author

Dr Gareth Moore is the best-selling author of over 150 puzzle and brain-training books for both children and adults, including *The Mindfulness Puzzle Book*, *The Mammoth Book of New Sudoku* and *The Ordnance Survey Puzzle Book*. His books have sold millions of copies worldwide.

He is also the creator of the daily brain-training website BrainedUp.com, and runs popular puzzle site PuzzleMix.com.

Web: **DrGarethMoore.com**
Twitter: **@DrGarethMoore**

Also by Dr Gareth Moore from the same publisher:

The Mindfulness Puzzle Book
The Mindfulness Puzzle Book 2
The Mindfulness Puzzle Book 3
The Mindfulness Puzzle Book 4
Mindfulness Puzzles For Your Kindle

The Great British Puzzle Book
The Beautiful Flower Dot-to-dot Book
The World Puzzle Championship Challenge
The RAF Association Puzzle Book

The Mammoth Book of Logical Brain Games
The Mammoth Book of Brain Games
The Mammoth Book of New Sudoku
The Mammoth Book of Fun Brain Training
The Mammoth Book of Brain Workouts

THE
ASTROLOGY
PUZZLE
BOOK

DR GARETH MOORE

ROBINSON

ROBINSON

First published in Great Britain in 2022 by Robinson

1 3 5 7 9 10 8 6 4 2

A CIP catalogue record for this book is available from the British
Library.

ISBN: 978-1-47214-774-5

Designed and typeset in Avenir LT by Dr Gareth Moore
Astrology icons: yosuke14 / Adobe Stock
Printed and bound in Great Britain by Clays Ltd, Elcograf S.p.A.

Papers used by Robinson are from well-managed forests and
other responsible sources.

Robinson
An imprint of
Little, Brown Book Group
Carmelite House
50 Victoria Embankment
London EC4Y 0DZ
An Hachette UK Company

www.hachette.co.uk

www.littlebrown.co.uk

CONTENTS

For all who reach
for the stars

INTRODUCTION

Welcome to *The Astrology Puzzle Book*, packed from cover to cover with a wide range of astrologically themed puzzles. Most of these are word puzzles but there are also some logic and picture puzzles, so there's something for everyone.

The puzzles are grouped by each of the twelve signs of the Zodiac, so you can either jump straight to your chosen sign or you can work your way through in order as you prefer. The puzzles are not arranged by difficulty, so if you find one too tricky then you can always just move on to the next – or take a look at the full solutions, at the back of the book, to get an extra clue to get you going.

Have fun!

Dr Gareth Moore

Rearrange these boxes to spell out seven words, all associated with Aries. Each box will be used exactly once.

AP	**CAR**	**CH**
DI	**ED**	**FI**
M	**MA**	**MAR**
NAL	**R**	**RA**
RE	**RIL**	**RS**

Place the capitalized surnames of these Aries celebrities into the grid once each, crossword style.

4 letters
Jackie CHAN
Celine DION
Lady GAGA
Elton JOHN
Diana ROSS
Paul RUDD

5 letters
Mariah CAREY

Dennis QUAID
Saoirse RONAN

6 letters
Eddie MURPHY

7 letters
David OYELOWO

8 letters
Ewan MCGREGOR
Pharrell WILLIAMS

9 letters
Keira KNIGHTLEY

11 letters
Reese
    WITHERSPOON

Reveal a word associated with those born under Aries by placing A, D, E, I, L, M, O, T or V into each empty square, so that no letter repeats in any row, column or bold-lined 3×3 box. Once solved, the word can be read down the shaded diagonal.

		D	E	T	I	V		
				L				
L			A		V			M
T		E				D		V
A	D						L	O
I		O				M		E
O			D		L			I
				I				
		I	O	A	T	L		

How many words can you find in this word square, including a nine-letter word that might describe an Aries? Make each word by starting on any letter square and then tracing a path to touching squares, including diagonally. Each word must be at least three letters in length, and a letter square can't be used more than once in a given word.

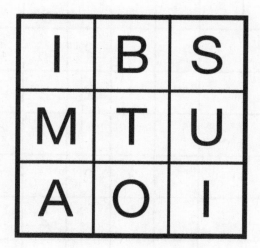

Targets:
Good: 15 words
Fantastic: 20 words

Can you find all the hidden stars in this grid? Clue numbers in some squares show the number of stars in touching squares – including diagonally. No more than one star can be placed per square, and there are no stars in the squares that contain numbers.

		1	2		2	
2	3			2		2
		2		2	2	
3	3					2
		3	3	3		1
	5				2	
2		3		3		1

Rearrange the letters within each column to reveal a quote about astrology, along with the person who it is attributed to. Words may be broken across lines, but every space is included no matter its position. Spaces are shown by empty boxes.

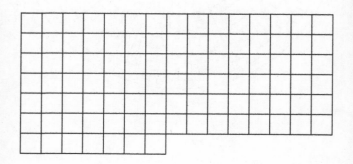

A	A	A	A	L	A	C	C	A	A	E	H	E	D	A
E	C	H	F	N	A	H	I	I	G	H	L	F	I	G
H	C	O	H	S	E	I	I	I	O	L	L	G	P	O
H	O	P	L	T	I	S	K	M	O	N	O	I	T	P
O	P	R	T	Y	O	S	R	N	N.	W	T	W	Y	T
	S	Y		S		T	R	S						
	U													

How quickly can you navigate your way to the centre of this star map?

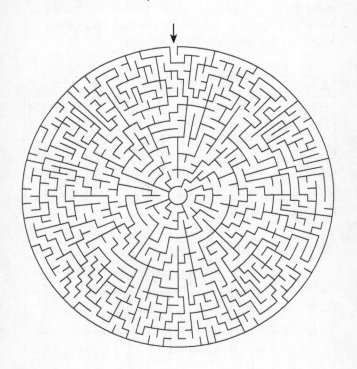

Crack the number-to-letter code by solving the
following clues, writing each clue's answer in
the squares beneath, with one letter per square.
Once you have solved the code, reveal the Aries
characteristic at the bottom of the page.

Goal:

4	6	5

Angry:

5	4	1

Full of wild excitement:

5	4	3	6	7

Night's opposite:

1	4	2

Might:

5	4	2

Aries characteristic:

1	2	3	4	5	6	7

Arians are known for a wide range of traits, including those listed below. Find them all in the word search, written in a straight line in any direction, including diagonally and backwards.

```
M C I T S I M I T P O E T
E O D E V I T R E S S A V
C M P E N N U U D L O B P
C P G R T E S P U E D R O
O E T E I E R F B T E E S
U T E S N T R G I E U O I
R I R O E E C M E U A T T
A T P I E N R E I T E T I
G I C H S U O O R N I T V
E V C I A M D H U I E C E
O E V I T A E R C S D D G
U A S E T A N O I S S A P
S A I M P U L S I V E R V
```

ASSERTIVE	ENERGETIC
BOLD	GENEROUS
CHEERFUL	HONEST
COMPETITIVE	IMPULSIVE
COURAGEOUS	OPTIMISTIC
CREATIVE	PASSIONATE
DETERMINED	POSITIVE
DIRECT	UPBEAT

Can you crack the letter-shift code to reveal the names of three stars found in the constellation of Aries?

Just as the light from distant stars shifts in colour as it travels to earth, so each letter has been shifted by a fixed amount. For example, A might have become B; B might have become C, and so on, wrapping around from Z back to A.

Leqep

Wlivexer

Qiwevxlmq

A	B	C	D	E	F	G	H	I	J	K	L	M

N	O	P	Q	R	S	T	U	V	W	X	Y	Z

Rearrange the order of the letters in each **capitalized** word to reveal five facts about the constellation of Aries.

- The name 'Aries' comes from the Latin word for **ARM**

- The constellation was once believed to depict a **FNADHARM**

- In Greek mythology, Aries **SECURED** the children of King Athamas

- Before becoming a constellation, Aries had a famous **LONGED** fleece

- Aries has sometimes been depicted with **SWING**

Join the stars in order to reveal a picture of Aries.

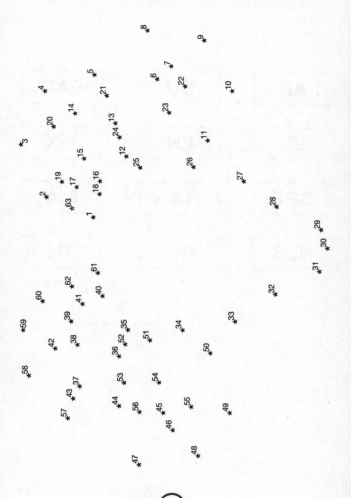

Rearrange these boxes to spell out seven words, all associated with Taurus. Each box will be used exactly once.

AP	BU	EAR
ED	EN	FIX
GRE	LL	MA
NUS	RIL	TH

VE	Y

Place the capitalized names of these Taurus celebrities into the grid once each, crossword style.

4 letters
Jessica ALBA
CHER

5 letters
ADELE
LIZZO
Channing TATUM

6 letters
Jamie DORNAN

7 letters
David BECKHAM
Janet JACKSON

8 letters
Kelly CLARKSON
Jerry SEINFELD

9 letters
Robert PATTINSON
Barbra STREISAND
Renee ZELLWEGER

Reveal a word associated with those born under Taurus by placing C, D, E, I, M, O, R, S or T into each empty square, so that no letter repeats in any row, column or bold-lined 3×3 box. Once solved, the word can be read down the shaded diagonal.

			O			R	M	
D			I		M	E		
I	T		S					
	D					S	I	T
M	C	I					R	
				I			C	R
		D	C		S			O
	R	C			O			

How many words can you find in this word square, including a nine-letter word that might describe a Taurus? Make each word by starting on any letter square and then tracing a path to touching squares, including diagonally. Each word must be at least three letters in length, and a letter square can't be used more than once in a given word.

Targets:
Good: 15 words
Fantastic: 25 words

23

Can you find all the hidden stars in this grid? Clue numbers in some squares show the number of stars in touching squares – including diagonally. No more than one star can be placed per square, and there are no stars in the squares that contain numbers.

1			1	2		1
	1	1		3	3	
2	2	2		3		
2					4	3
2			5	3		
	4				4	2
		2	4		3	

Rearrange the letters within each column to reveal a quote about astrology, along with the person who it is attributed to. Words may be broken across lines, but every space is included no matter its position. Spaces are shown by empty boxes.

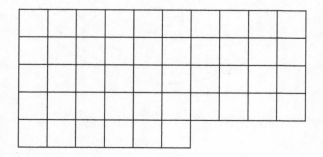

How quickly can you navigate your way to the centre of this star map?

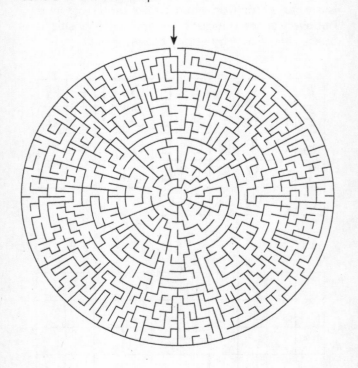

Crack the number-to-letter code by solving the following clues, writing each clue's answer in the squares beneath, with one letter per square. Once you have solved the code, reveal the Taurus characteristic at the bottom of the page.

Love:

1	8	5	6	7	

Deserve:

7	1	6	2

Idol:

4	7	6	5

Encryption:

3	5	8	7

Nurture

3	1	6	7

Taurus characteristic:

1	2	3	4	5	6	7	8

Taureans are known for a wide range of traits, including those listed below. Find them all in the word search, written in a straight line in any direction, including diagonally and backwards.

```
T N E I L I S E R E T W R
B G R O U N D E D T G Y E
L U F H T I A F S N P H L
G C A O T N S E I E E T B
S U O N C T O K R L R R A
S U H N R U R D T B S O D
T N O O S O S N E A I W N
A S N I W I E E L I S T E
B G D D C G S A D L T S P
L N R I I A Y T O E E U E
E A U L T O N T E R N R D
H T I L L I S E E N T T D
D D N R O B B U T S T P B
```

CONSISTENT
DEPENDABLE
DILIGENT
FAITHFUL
FOCUSED
GROUNDED
HARD-WORKING
LOYAL

PERSISTENT
RELIABLE
RESILIENT
STABLE
STRONG
STUBBORN
TENACIOUS
TRUSTWORTHY

Can you crack the letter-shift code to reveal the names of three stars found in the constellation of Taurus?

Just as the light from distant stars shifts in colour as it travels to earth, so each letter has been shifted by a fixed amount. For example, A might have become B; B might have become C, and so on, wrapping around from Z back to A.

Cnfgdctcp

Jacfgu

Rngkcfgu

A	B	C	D	E	F	G	H	I	J	K	L	M

N	O	P	Q	R	S	T	U	V	W	X	Y	Z

Rearrange the order of the letters in each **capitalized** word to reveal five facts about the constellation of Taurus.

- Taurus may have been depicted as a bull in early **VECA** paintings

- The constellation features a star cluster known as the Seven **RESISTS**

- Ancient Egyptians saw Taurus as a sign of new life in **GRIPSN**

- In Greek mythology, Taurus may represent the Cretan bull which created the **AIRMOUNT**

- In Inuit mythology, the constellation contains a star which represents a hunted **LOPRA** bear

Join the stars in order to reveal a picture of Taurus.

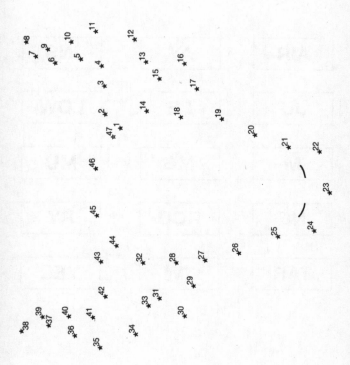

Rearrange these boxes to spell out seven words, all associated with Gemini. Each box will be used exactly once.

AIR	AY	INS
JU	LE	LOW
M	ME	MU
NE	RCU	RY
TAB	TW	YEL

Place the capitalized names of these Gemini celebrities into the grid once each, crossword style.

3 letters
Laverne COX

4 letters
Lauryn HILL

5 letters
Angelina JOLIE

6 letters
Nicole KIDMAN
Idina MENZEL
Marilyn MONROE
PRINCE

7 letters
Colin FARRELL
Morgan FREEMAN
Tom HOLLAND

Natalie PORTMAN
Aly RAISMAN
Octavia SPENCER

8 letters
Ian MCKELLEN

Reveal a word associated with those born under Gemini by placing C, D, E, I, N, R, S, T or V into each empty square, so that no letter repeats in any row, column or bold-lined 3×3 box. Once solved, the word can be read down the shaded diagonal.

		T		N				
		I	V		C			
			T				C	I
	I			V		T	R	
D			C		N			S
	S	V		E			I	
E	R				V			
			I		E	D		
				C		S		

How many words can you find in this word square, including a nine-letter word that might describe a Gemini? Make each word by starting on any letter square and then tracing a path to touching squares, including diagonally. Each word must be at least three letters in length, and a letter square can't be used more than once in a given word.

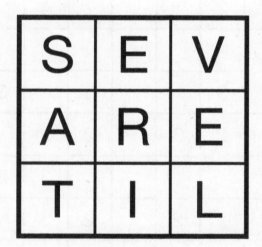

Targets:
Good: 40 words
Fantastic: 55 words

Can you find all the hidden stars in this grid? Clue numbers in some squares show the number of stars in touching squares – including diagonally. No more than one star can be placed per square, and there are no stars in the squares that contain numbers.

1	2			2	4	
1			4			
	3			3		3
	2	3		2	2	
1					3	2
2		2		2	3	
	2		2		2	1

Rearrange the letters within each column to reveal a quote about astrology, along with the person who it is attributed to. Words may be broken across lines, but every space is included no matter its position. Spaces are shown by empty boxes.

H	B	A	A	A	A	D	E	A	B	E	C	E	C	A
M.	D	A	B	H	E	L	E	D	R	E	H	I	H	E
N	E	J	L	L	N	R	M	E	R	E	L	K	I	H
W	E		O	R	N		S	E	S	S	N	N	R	S
	W		S	T	P		S'	T	T	U	T	T		T
			Y		S,		W			W		Y		

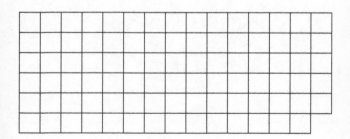

How quickly can you navigate your way to the centre of this star map?

Crack the number-to-letter code by solving the following clues, writing each clue's answer in the squares beneath, with one letter per square. Once you have solved the code, reveal the Gemini characteristic at the bottom of the page.

Greek god:

1	2	6	7

Ocean:

7	2	3

Spirit:

7	5	6	4

Manipulate:

6	7	2

Singular:

7	5	4	2

Gemini characteristic:

1	2	3	4	5	6	7

Geminians are known for a wide range of traits, including those listed below. Find them all in the word search, written in a straight line in any direction, including diagonally and backwards.

```
Y E E X P R E S S I V E I
E T X S O C I A L A I S E
Y N T T E U O N N F U O I
P E T I R A T A E O C N C
L E A H W O L G I P Q S E
A R R G U Y V C O U O C L
Y F E C T S A E I I U I B
F E O I E U I S R R N Y A
U R C S Q P I A I T T G T
L A H O L T T O S L E X P
L C L E I I U I O T X D A
E P E V C S O I V U I G D
F L E X I B L E L E I C A
```

ADAPTABLE	INQUISITIVE
ANALYTICAL	LOQUACIOUS
CAREFREE	OPEN
CURIOUS	OUTGOING
ENTHUSIASTIC	PERCEPTIVE
EXPRESSIVE	PLAYFUL
EXTROVERTED	SOCIAL
FLEXIBLE	WITTY

Can you crack the letter-shift code to reveal the names of three stars found in the constellation of Gemini?

Just as the light from distant stars shifts in colour as it travels to earth, so each letter has been shifted by a fixed amount. For example, A might have become B; B might have become C, and so on, wrapping around from Z back to A.

Xwttcf

Kiabwz

Itpmvi

A	B	C	D	E	F	G	H	I	J	K	L	M

N	O	P	Q	R	S	T	U	V	W	X	Y	Z

Rearrange the order of the letters in each **capitalized** word to reveal five facts about the constellation of Gemini.

- The stars Castor and Pollux are referred to in Babylonian mythology as the Great **SWINT**

- They were both said to be depictions of the Babylonian god of the **DROWNRULED**

- In Greek mythology, Pollux asked that his brother be made **RIOTLAMM**, so Zeus turned them into stars

- The pair are considered to be the protectors of **SOLARIS**

- They are often depicted riding **SHORES**

Join the stars in order to reveal a picture of Gemini.

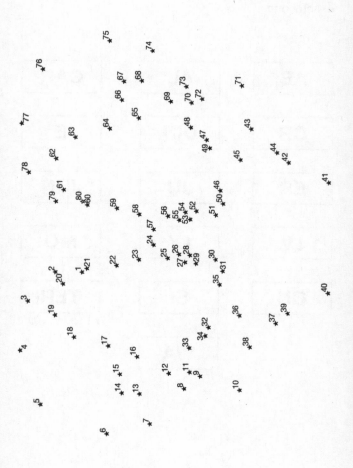

Rearrange these boxes to spell out seven words, all associated with Cancer. Each box will be used exactly once.

AB	AL	CAR
CR	DIN	E
ER	JU	JUN
LV	LY	MO
ON	SI	TER
	WA	

Place the capitalized surnames of these Cancer celebrities into the grid once each, crossword style.

2 letters
Sandra OH

4 letters
Harrison FORD
Elon MUSK

5 letters
Kevin BACON
Tom HANKS
Ringo STARR

6 letters
Tom CRUISE
Ariana GRANDE
Mindy KALING
Meryl STREEP

7 letters
Sofia VERGARA

8 letters
Nick OFFERMAN
Forest WHITAKER

Reveal a word associated with those born under
Cancer by placing A, D, G, I, N, R, S, T or U into
each empty square, so that no letter repeats in any
row, column or bold-lined 3×3 box. Once solved,
the word can be read down the shaded diagonal.

	G						I	
		T		D		N		
			A	G	N			
	S	U				D	A	
A								I
	T	D				G	S	
			U	S	A			
		I		R		U		
	R						D	

How many words can you find in this word square, including a nine-letter word that might describe a Cancer? Make each word by starting on any letter square and then tracing a path to touching squares, including diagonally. Each word must be at least three letters in length, and a letter square can't be used more than once in a given word.

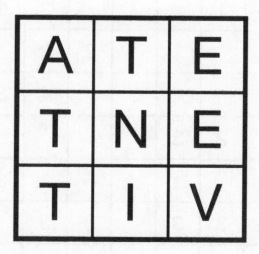

Targets:
Good: 15 words
Fantastic: 20 words

Can you find all the hidden stars in this grid? Clue numbers in some squares show the number of stars in touching squares – including diagonally. No more than one star can be placed per square, and there are no stars in the squares that contain numbers.

	1		2		2	1
2		1		2	2	
			3		4	3
2	2	3				
1				5		3
	3	3		3	3	
	2		2		2	

Rearrange the letters within each column to reveal a quote about astrology, along with the person who it is attributed to. Words may be broken across lines, but every space is included no matter its position. Spaces are shown by empty boxes.

H	E	E	A	D	E	A	A	M	O	A	B	A
H	F	E	A	I	F	H	L	O	O	E	D	E
I	F	H	I	L	G	I	L	S	S	F	O	O
T	H	O	N	R	L	U	R	T	S	T	R	T
		W	N	S	L	Y	T.		V			
			V	T								

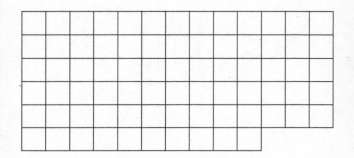

How quickly can you navigate your way to the centre of this star map?

Crack the number-to-letter code by solving the
following clues, writing each clue's answer in
the squares beneath, with one letter per square.
Once you have solved the code, reveal the Cancer
characteristic at the bottom of the page.

Pleasant:

2	3	8	1

Supernatural:

5	6	4	3	8

Jewel:

4	1	5

Visualize:

3	5	6	4	3	2	1

Attractive:

5	6	4	2	1	7	3	8

Cancer characteristic:

1	2	3	4	5	6	7	3	8

Cancerians are known for a wide range of traits, including those listed below. Find them all in the word search, written in a straight line in any direction, including diagonally and backwards.

```
I V E S E N S I T I V E T
C S L I E M O T I O N A L
I I U C I T E H T A P M E
G D N O D D M L O Y A L S
L G E T I E E O E V G Y S
A O N T U R T R T O L E E
T E V I O I E T E R A L L
S E A I R V T T I Y E T F
O T N E N A E I S M A O L
N M O M L G C D V Y M L E
I G E N E R O U S E M O S
G P R O T E C T I V E A C
A N S E N T I M E N T A L
```

CARING	LOVING
COMMITTED	LOYAL
DEVOTED	MYSTERIOUS
EMOTIONAL	NOSTALGIC
EMPATHETIC	PROTECTIVE
GENEROUS	SELFLESS
INTUITIVE	SENSITIVE
LAYERED	SENTIMENTAL

Can you crack the letter-shift code to reveal the names of three stars found in the constellation of Cancer?

Just as the light from distant stars shifts in colour as it travels to earth, so each letter has been shifted by a fixed amount. For example, A might have become B; B might have become C, and so on, wrapping around from Z back to A.

Wdui

Dfxehqv

Whjplqh

A	B	C	D	E	F	G	H	I	J	K	L	M

N	O	P	Q	R	S	T	U	V	W	X	Y	Z

Rearrange the order of the letters in each
capitalized word to reveal five facts about the
constellation of Cancer.

- The constellation of Cancer was recorded
  by the **MOONSTARER** Ptolemy, though
  he gave it the Greek name Karkinos

- The giant crab Karkinos is supposed to
  have bitten the hero **LEECRUSH** during
  his twelve tasks

- The Greek goddess **RHEA** placed the
  crab into the sky as a reward

- In Ancient Babylonia, the constellation
  may have been interpreted as a **LUTTER**

- Ancient Egyptians referred to the
  constellation as a **CRABAS** beetle

Join the stars in order to reveal a picture of Cancer.

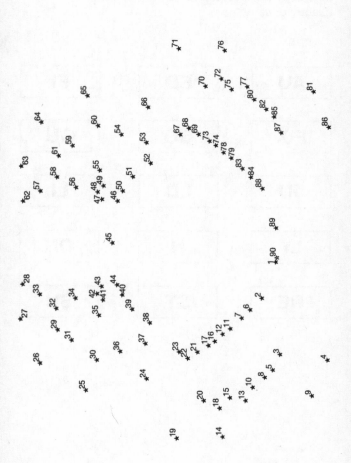

Rearrange these boxes to spell out seven words, all associated with Leo. Each box will be used exactly once.

AU	ED	FI
FIX	GO	GU
JU	LD	LI
LY	N	ON
RE	ST	SU

Place the capitalized surnames of these Leo celebrities into the grid once each, crossword style.

5 letters
Amy ADAMS
Halle BERRY
Viola DAVIS
Mila KUNIS
Jennifer LOPEZ
Jason MOMOA
Barack OBAMA

6 letters
Robert DE NIRO
Mick JAGGER
Demi LOVATO
Helen MIRREN

7 letters
Matt LEBLANC
MADONNA
Maya RUDOLPH

8 letters
Antonio
  BANDERAS

9 letters
Chris
  HEMSWORTH

57

Reveal a word associated with those born under Leo by placing A, C, D, E, F, I, N, O or T into each empty square, so that no letter repeats in any row, column or bold-lined 3×3 box. Once solved, the word can be read down the shaded diagonal.

	E		D				T	
T		A		C				F
	F				I		E	
O						A		
	D				C		F	
		T		E				I
			I					
E		D		T				O
	C				N		A	

How many words can you find in this word square, including a nine-letter word that might describe a Leo? Make each word by starting on any letter square and then tracing a path to touching squares, including diagonally. Each word must be at least three letters in length, and a letter square can't be used more than once in a given word.

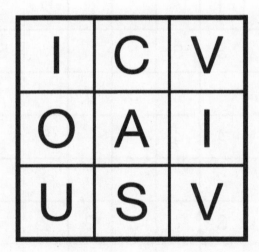

Targets:
Good: 4 words
Fantastic: 6 words

Can you find all the hidden stars in this grid? Clue numbers in some squares show the number of stars in touching squares – including diagonally. No more than one star can be placed per square, and there are no stars in the squares that contain numbers.

	1			2	2	
2	3	3				3
2			5	5		
	4	4			5	
	2				4	
	3		3	2	2	
1				1	1	1

Rearrange the letters within each column to reveal a quote about astrology, along with the person who it is attributed to. Words may be broken across lines, but every space is included no matter its position. Spaces are shown by empty boxes.

E	A	E	A	A	E	A	L	E	E	A	D	D	A	D
E	E	E,	D	G	L	D	L	F	O	A	H	I	N	H
H	H	N	I	L	N		O	O	T	I	N	O	T	T
I	S	P	I	N	N		R	R		K	T	Y		
L		T		O	T			S		T				
T		W		S	Y.									

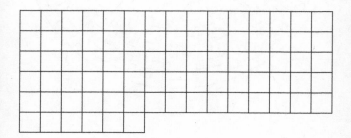

How quickly can you navigate your way to the centre of this star map?

Crack the number-to-letter code by solving the following clues, writing each clue's answer in the squares beneath, with one letter per square. Once you have solved the code, reveal the Leo characteristic at the bottom of the page.

Outpouring:

6	8	2	3

Unsullied:

1	7	5	4

Pelt:

6	7	5

Roam, as a lion:

1	5	2	3	8

The constellation *Lupus*:

3	2	8	6

Leo characteristic:

1	2	3	4	5	6	7	8

Leos are known for a wide range of traits, including those listed below. Find them all in the word search, written in a straight line in any direction, including diagonally and backwards.

```
L I A S R S T R I K I N G
N P C C S U O R E N E G C
U N R A T N F E V T R R D
F A U O P I E Y P T A E S
E G S C U T V V H C R J U
V K N A Y D I E I U R O O
I F R I G L A V S R S Y R
T U N A T T E S A R D F O
A I H C R S A V E T O U M
E A D I R F U I I O I L U
R U C I L P S R L L N N H
C A L E V A R B T U R I G
L E S L U F T C E P S E R
```

ACTIVE	JOYFUL
BRAVE	LIVELY
CAPTIVATING	PROUD
CREATIVE	RESPECTFUL
DRIVEN	SELF-ASSURED
FUN	STRIKING
GENEROUS	THEATRICAL
HUMOROUS	TRUSTING

Can you crack the letter-shift code to reveal the names of three stars found in the constellation of Leo?

Just as the light from distant stars shifts in colour as it travels to earth, so each letter has been shifted by a fixed amount. For example, A might have become B; B might have become C, and so on, wrapping around from Z back to A.

Boqevec

Noxolyvk

Jycwk

A	B	C	D	E	F	G	H	I	J	K	L	M

N	O	P	Q	R	S	T	U	V	W	X	Y	Z

Rearrange the order of the letters in each **capitalized** word to reveal five facts about the constellation of Leo.

- Leo's star, **SLUGRUE**, is one of the brightest in the night sky

- The lion is said to be the one killed in the **RIFTS** of the twelve labours of a Greek hero

- According to the myth, the ferocious lion could not be harmed by any **APENOW**

- In Ancient Sumer, the constellation was said to depict a **MENTORS** killed by Gilgamesh

- The constellation features a curved string of stars known as the **LICKES**

Join the stars in order to reveal a picture of Leo.

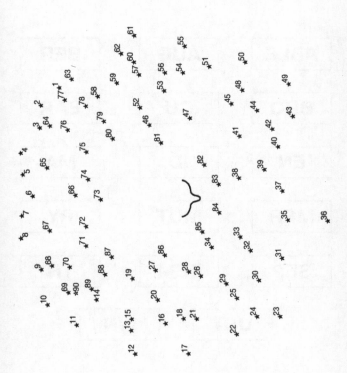

Rearrange these boxes to spell out seven words, all associated with Virgo. Each box will be used exactly once.

ABLE	AUG	BER
BRO	CU	EAR
EN	ID	MA
MER	MUT	RY
SEP	TEM	TH

UST	WN

Place the capitalized names of these Virgo celebrities into the grid once each, crossword style.

4 letters
Cameron DIAZ
Idris ELBA
Richard GERE
Chris PINE

5 letters
Jack BLACK
Michael BUBLÉ
Salma HAYEK

Nick JONAS
Shania TWAIN

6 letters
Alexis BLEDEL
Jennifer HUDSON
Blake LIVELY
Keanu REEVES

7 letters
BEYONCE
Gloria ESTEFAN
Adam SANDLER
ZENDAYA

Reveal a word associated with those born under Virgo by placing A, C, E, I, L, P, R, S or T into each empty square, so that no letter repeats in any row, column or bold-lined 3×3 box. Once solved, the word can be read down the shaded diagonal.

	S		A				C	
I		T						A
	C		I					
L		E		S				
			P		R			
				E		A		P
					L		E	
S						T		I
	E				C		R	

How many words can you find in this word square, including a nine-letter word that might describe a Virgo? Make each word by starting on any letter square and then tracing a path to touching squares, including diagonally. Each word must be at least three letters in length, and a letter square can't be used more than once in a given word.

Targets:
Good: 20 words
Fantastic: 30 words

Can you find all the hidden stars in this grid? Clue numbers in some squares show the number of stars in touching squares – including diagonally. No more than one star can be placed per square, and there are no stars in the squares that contain numbers.

	2	2	2			1
3					3	
				1		3
3	5	3		3	5	
			2			
	3	3		3	5	
1		2		1	2	

Rearrange the letters within each column to reveal a quote about astrology, along with the person who it is attributed to. Words may be broken across lines, but every space is included no matter its position. Spaces are shown by empty boxes.

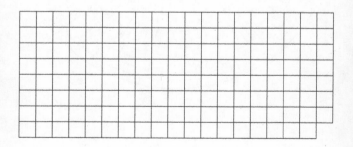

A	C	D	E	E	E	A	H	A	I	A	A	E	E	D	E	E	A	E
E	M	I	E	E	E	A	I	A	I	T	E	F	E	I	G	I	C	H
E	O	K	H	N	O	F	I	E	S	T	H	G	I	N	H	P	H	H
O	T	O	O	N,	Q	L	I	F	S	T	L	L	I	N	I	T	I	H
S	U	S	O	O	R	R	O	S	S		O	O	L	O	P	V	I	N
	T	R	T		T	R	T	S.		O	P	R	R	R	Y	T	R
	Y	R	Y		U	S	U	T		R	W		S	S		T	T
		S										T					

How quickly can you navigate your way to the centre of this star map?

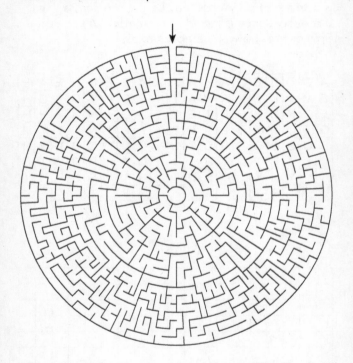

Crack the number-to-letter code by solving the
following clues, writing each clue's answer in
the squares beneath, with one letter per square.
Once you have solved the code, reveal the Virgo
characteristic at the bottom of the page.

Correct:

7	1	6	2

Outcome:

1	2	3	6	5	7

Reigns:

1	6	5	2	3

Collection:

3	2	7

Pathways:

1	4	6	7	2	3

Virgo characteristic:

1	2	3	4	5	6	7	2

Virgoans are known for a wide range of traits, including those listed below. Find them all in the word search, written in a straight line in any direction, including diagonally and backwards.

```
S T M E T I C U L O U S C
A N L A U T I B A H E T S
T E P P R U C M N V L U L
T I T P U P O S I U O U A
E C N E U D U T F I F E C
N I S U E O C E R E L N I
T F O S I U S T C B S E D
I F T D D O S R I I I C O
V E U O P U U S E F O P H
E T R R D O N D N I K N T
S P U N S E H U M B L E E
S P I E S T N E D U R P M
M M R R A L U C I T R A P
```

ATTENTIVE
EFFICIENT
HABITUAL
HUMBLE
INDUSTRIOUS
KIND
METHODICAL
METICULOUS

MODEST
PARTICULAR
PRODUCTIVE
PRUDENT
PURPOSEFUL
RESOURCEFUL
SENSIBLE
STUDIOUS

Can you crack the letter-shift code to reveal the names of three stars found in the constellation of Virgo?

Just as the light from distant stars shifts in colour as it travels to earth, so each letter has been shifted by a fixed amount. For example, A might have become B; B might have become C, and so on, wrapping around from Z back to A.

Xunhf

Utwwnrf

Mjej

A	B	C	D	E	F	G	H	I	J	K	L	M

N	O	P	Q	R	S	T	U	V	W	X	Y	Z

Rearrange the order of the letters in each
capitalized word to reveal five facts about the
constellation of Virgo.

- Virgo is the **STARLEG** constellation in the
zodiac

- Some cultures have depicted Virgo as a
maiden, holding a set of **CLASSE**

- Virgo is associated with the goddess
Persephone, who was kidnapped
by **SHADE** and taken to the Greek
underworld

- The maiden Virgo is frequently
associated with **ATHEW**

- Babylonian depictions of Virgo are
interpreted as a goddess holding a
LAMP leaf

Join the stars in order to reveal a picture of Virgo.

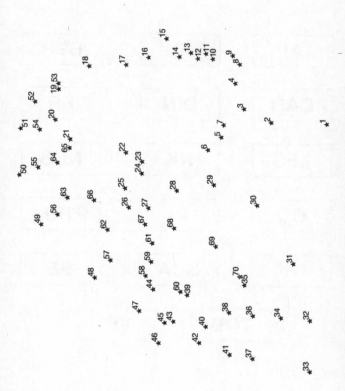

Rearrange these boxes to spell out seven words, all associated with Libra. Each box will be used exactly once.

AI	AL	BER
CAR	DIN	ER
LES	NK	NUS
OC	PI	PTEM
R	SCA	SE
TOB	VE	

Place the capitalized surnames of these Libra celebrities into the grid once each, crossword style.

4 letters
Snoop DOGG
Bruno MARS

5 letters
Zac EFRON

6 letters
Donald GLOVER

7 letters
Julie ANDREWS
Hugh JACKMAN
Gwen STEFANI
Kate WINSLET

8 letters
Jeff GOLDBLUM
Serena WILLIAMS

9 letters
John KRASINSKI

10 letters
Kim KARDASHIAN

Reveal a word associated with those born under
Libra by placing C, D, E, I, L, P, R, T or V into each
empty square, so that no letter repeats in any row,
column or bold-lined 3×3 box. Once solved, the
word can be read down the shaded diagonal.

	T		C				E	
V		P		T				I
	L				V			
T						P		
	R						L	
		I				C		V
			P		E		D	
C				L		R		P
	I				D		T	

How many words can you find in this word square, including a nine-letter word that might describe a Libra? Make each word by starting on any letter square and then tracing a path to touching squares, including diagonally. Each word must be at least three letters in length, and a letter square can't be used more than once in a given word.

Targets:
Good: 25 words
Fantastic: 40 words

Can you find all the hidden stars in this grid? Clue numbers in some squares show the number of stars in touching squares – including diagonally. No more than one star can be placed per square, and there are no stars in the squares that contain numbers.

	1	1	1	2		1
2				3	2	2
	1		2			1
1	1	1	2		2	
1	1			4		1
1			3			3
	2		2	3		

Rearrange the letters within each column to reveal a quote about astrology, along with the person who it is attributed to. Words may be broken across lines, but every space is included no matter its position. Spaces are shown by empty boxes.

E	E	D	D	A	N	E	I	A	E	A	D	H	L	A
G	F	I	H	E	N	N	R	A	L	B	E.	O	L	G
H	I	O	I	G	N	O	R	E,	N	C	G	O	T	H
K	T	T	I	M	U	T	T	I	S	I	N	S,	T	O
O	Y		M	O	W	T	W	R		I	R		U	U
S			N			S		T	R					
W			T											

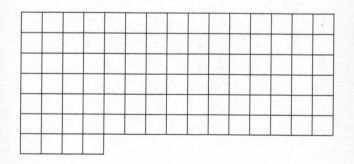

How quickly can you navigate your way to the centre of this star map?

Crack the number-to-letter code by solving the following clues, writing each clue's answer in the squares beneath, with one letter per square. Once you have solved the code, reveal the Libra characteristic at the bottom of the page.

Libra sign:

3	5	2

Dawn goddess:

3	7	2	6	2	3

Epic:

8	3	1	3

Inquisitive:

4	7	2	5	6	7	8

Major problem:

4	2	5	8	5	8

Libra characteristic:

1	2	3	4	5	6	7	8

Librans are known for a wide range of traits, including those listed below. Find them all in the word search, written in a straight line in any direction, including diagonally and backwards.

```
O C O O P E R A T I V E C
C I T A M O L P I D R R A
E Y C Y T T I W J E I C I
A A D O E J P H S A I Y A
S R N I N S U P F T D L S
Y L Y L U S O S E Y E R P
G E U A A N I H T U C E O
O A V F S R T D N C N D R
I E E I T A O A E S A R T
N O B L P C C M E R L O I
G L I M T I A T R L A E N
E N E C L S T T S D B T G
S I D E A L I S T I C R E
```

BALANCED	JUST
CONSIDERATE	MORAL
COOPERATIVE	ORDERLY
DIPLOMATIC	RESPONSIBLE
EASY-GOING	SPORTING
EMPATHETIC	SUAVE
FAIR	TACTFUL
IDEALISTIC	WITTY

Can you crack the letter-shift code to reveal the names of three stars found in the constellation of Libra?

Just as the light from distant stars shifts in colour as it travels to earth, so each letter has been shifted by a fixed amount. For example, A might have become B; B might have become C, and so on, wrapping around from Z back to A.

Gbilulsnlubip

Gbilulzjohthsp

Iyhjopbt

A	B	C	D	E	F	G	H	I	J	K	L	M

N	O	P	Q	R	S	T	U	V	W	X	Y	Z

Rearrange the order of the letters in each **capitalized** word to reveal five facts about the constellation of Libra.

- The scales are associated with Astraea, the goddess of **CUTIESJ**

- Several civilizations have characterized the scales as a pair of **COINSPOR** claws

- The connection to balance may be linked to Libra's connection to the **UMLAUTAN** equinox

- Ancient Egyptians interpreted Libra's three brightest stars as forming the shape of a **TABO**

- Libra is the only astrological sign whose symbol is an **INNATEAIM** object

Join the stars in order to reveal a picture of Libra.

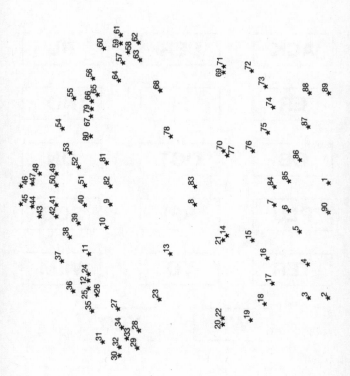

Rearrange these boxes to spell out seven words, all associated with Scorpio. Each box will be used exactly once.

ACK	BER	BL
ER	FI	NO
OB	OCT	ON
PLU	RPI	SCO
TER	TO	VEM
	WA	XED

Place the capitalized surnames of these Scorpio celebrities into the grid once each, crossword style.

5 letters
Sean COMBS
DRAKE
Sally FIELD
Bill GATES
Demi MOORE
Winona RYDER
Emma STONE

6 letters
Danny DEVITO
Jodie FOSTER
Owen WILSON

7 letters
Ryan GOSLING
Pablo PICASSO
Julia ROBERTS

8 letters
Leonardo DICAPRIO
Whoopi GOLDBERG

Reveal a word associated with those born under
Scorpio by placing C, D, E, I, L, R, S, T or V into
each empty square, so that no letter repeats in any
row, column or bold-lined 3×3 box. Once solved,
the word can be read down the shaded diagonal.

		R	C				I	
L		D						
				R	E		D	S
		I		S				T
		L	I		C	V		
E				D		L		
C	S		E	L				
						S		C
		I			V	R		

How many words can you find in this word square, including a nine-letter word that might describe a Scorpio? Make each word by starting on any letter square and then tracing a path to touching squares, including diagonally. Each word must be at least three letters in length, and a letter square can't be used more than once in a given word.

Targets:
Good: 20 words
Fantastic: 30 words

Can you find all the hidden stars in this grid? Clue numbers in some squares show the number of stars in touching squares – including diagonally. No more than one star can be placed per square, and there are no stars in the squares that contain numbers.

1		1		1	2	
2		3	2			2
		3			2	
1	2		4		4	3
	2	4				
2					5	4
	2	2		2		

Rearrange the letters within each column to reveal a quote about astrology, along with the person who it is attributed to. Words may be broken across lines, but every space is included no matter its position. Spaces are shown by empty boxes.

A	E	E	A	B	A	C	A	E	B	A	B	A	E	E	B	H	E
H	E	E	E	D	O	F	D.	M	E	F	H	E	F	I	E	M	E
K	H	K	I	E	O	L	L	R	J	L	H	F	H	M	O	N	E
N	H	P	L	O	R	R	N	T	O	N	I	I	N	N	O	S	M
T	L	T	W	P	R	T	O		R	O		O	N	T	S	Y	T
T	R	Y		R	S	U	O			S		T			T		
W	S			S		T			T		Y						
	T			T													

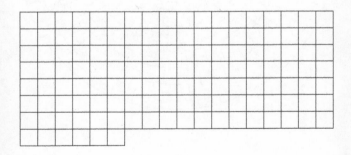

How quickly can you navigate your way to the centre of this star map?

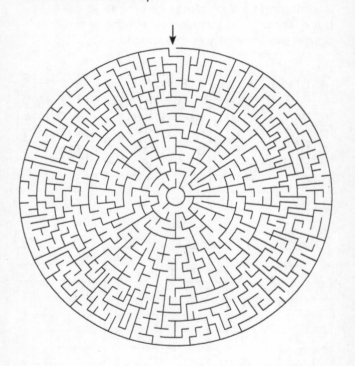

Crack the number-to-letter code by solving the following clues, writing each clue's answer in the squares beneath, with one letter per square. Once you have solved the code, reveal the Scorpio characteristic at the bottom of the page.

Goals:

1	4	2	8

Goal-setter:

3	6	8	8

Maxim:

2	6	5	5	6

Maximum:

7	5	2	6	8	5

Brag:

3	6	1	8	5

Scorpio characteristic:

1	2	3	4	5	4	6	7	8

Scorpians are known for a wide range of traits, including those listed below. Find them all in the word search, written in a straight line in any direction, including diagonally and backwards.

```
D R S I N T U I T I V E E
E N V U H E I G C O O L N
T V U G O O V A A T I T T
A B E O N I N I O H L R I
V R R V F I R E S I L Y C
I U I A I O D E S A O U I
T T S O V T R N T T V D N
O H I M O E P P A S U E G
M L S R V O I E N M Y E N
F E A R L E S S C C M M R
U S G N I R A D F R T O N
S S V C O M P L E X E E C
G F O R T H R I G H T P R
```

BRAVE
COMMANDING
COMPLEX
COOL
DARING
ENTICING
EVASIVE
FEARLESS

FORTHRIGHT
HONEST
INTUITIVE
MOTIVATED
MYSTERIOUS
PERCEPTIVE
PROFOUND
RUTHLESS

Can you crack the letter-shift code to reveal the names of three stars found in the constellation of Scorpio?

Just as the light from distant stars shifts in colour as it travels to earth, so each letter has been shifted by a fixed amount. For example, A might have become B; B might have become C, and so on, wrapping around from Z back to A.

Wftqfsujmjp

Tibvmb

Tbshbt

A	B	C	D	E	F	G	H	I	J	K	L	M

N	O	P	Q	R	S	T	U	V	W	X	Y	Z

Rearrange the order of the letters in each **capitalized** word to reveal five facts about the constellation of Scorpio.

- The Scorpian stars Shaula and Lesath both have names which mean **GNIST**

- In Greek mythology, the scorpion was sent to challenge the hunter **IRONO**, and both were made into constellations

- The scorpion was supposedly sent by the hunter goddess **MAESTRI**

- Some Hawaiians interpret the constellation as the **SHIF-KOHO** of the demigod Maui

- In Javanese Indonesia, the constellation's name refers to its similarity to a **TOONCUC** tree

Join the stars in order to reveal a picture of Scorpio.

Rearrange these boxes to spell out seven words, all associated with Sagittarius. Each box will be used exactly once.

ARC	BER	DEC
EM	EMB	ER
FI	HER	ITER
JUP	LE	MU
NOV	PLE	PUR
	RE	TAB

Place the capitalized surnames of these Sagittarius celebrities into the grid once each, crossword style.

3 letters
Lucy LIU

4 letters
Jamie FOXX
Jonah HILL
Eugene LEVY

5 letters
Miley CYRUS
Judi DENCH

Jane FONDA
Taylor SWIFT

6 letters
Britney SPEARS
Tina TURNER

7 letters
Jeff BRIDGES
Samuel L
  JACKSON

Zoe KRAVITZ
Ben STILLER

8 letters
Christina
  AGUILERA

9 letters
Steven
  SPIELBERG

Reveal a word associated with those born under Sagittarius by placing A, C, E, I, K, L, O, T or V into each empty square, so that no letter repeats in any row, column or bold-lined 3×3 box. Once solved, the word can be read down the shaded diagonal.

	V		E		K		A	
O				C				V
			O		A			
I		A				O		C
	L						K	
C		K				V		A
			V		C			
E				T				K
	O		A		I		T	

How many words can you find in this word square, including a nine-letter word that might describe a Sagittarius? Make each word by starting on any letter square and then tracing a path to touching squares, including diagonally. Each word must be at least three letters in length, and a letter square can't be used more than once in a given word.

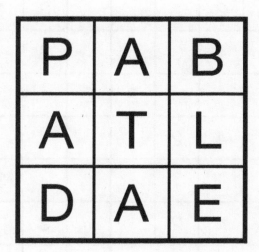

Targets:
Good: 15 words
Fantastic: 25 words

Can you find all the hidden stars in this grid? Clue numbers in some squares show the number of stars in touching squares – including diagonally. No more than one star can be placed per square, and there are no stars in the squares that contain numbers.

	2				3	1
2	4	3	5		3	
			2	2		3
2	4	2				
						3
2	4	2			2	
	2			1	2	1

Rearrange the letters within each column to reveal a quote about astrology, along with the person who it is attributed to. Words may be broken across lines, but every space is included no matter its position. Spaces are shown by empty boxes.

E	A	E	E.	B	A	A	H	A	E	A	A	A	E	A
L	E	F	R	E	H	A	O	C	E	A	M	B	F	H
R	E	O	R	M	O	C	S	P	N	H	S	N	H	I
T	H	P		O	S	E	T	S	R	O	T	O		O
T	H	R		T	V	I		R	O		O		T	
V	I	R				N			T			S		
	L													

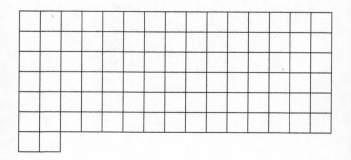

How quickly can you navigate your way to the centre of this star map?

Crack the number-to-letter code by solving the following clues, writing each clue's answer in the squares beneath, with one letter per square. Once you have solved the code, reveal the Sagittarius characteristic at the bottom of the page.

Entertaining:

4	1	2

Distant:

3	4	3	5

Ambience:

3	1	5	3

Celtic priest:

7	5	1	6	7

Passing trend:

4	3	7

Sagittarius characteristic:

1	2	3	4	5	3	6	7

Sagittarians are known for a wide range of traits, including those listed below. Find them all in the word search, written in a straight line in any direction, including diagonally and backwards.

```
A S P O N T A N E O U S I
S D G N O R T S D A E H L
U C V C R E A T I V E A I
O H P E P E S N I N N D N
I A I T N M T T C O I E D
L R E B A T A O I P K B E
L M E R I R U T E O A R P
E I T P O R A R P S E A E
B N E L A R T S O O O Z N
E G P G I N T E S U A E D
R X I P I U O O O O S N E
E N S U O M O N O T U A N
G A R C O N F I D E N T T
```

ADVENTUROUS
ASPIRATIONAL
AUTONOMOUS
BRAZEN
CHARMING
CONFIDENT
CREATIVE
ENCOURAGING

EXPLORATIVE
HEADSTRONG
INDEPENDENT
INTREPID
OUTSPOKEN
REBELLIOUS
SMART
SPONTANEOUS

Can you crack the letter-shift code to reveal the names of three stars found in the constellation of Sagittarius?

Just as the light from distant stars shifts in colour as it travels to earth, so each letter has been shifted by a fixed amount. For example, A might have become B; B might have become C, and so on, wrapping around from Z back to A.

Wdwtr

Jblnuuj

Yxurb

A	B	C	D	E	F	G	H	I	J	K	L	M

N	O	P	Q	R	S	T	U	V	W	X	Y	Z

Rearrange the order of the letters in each **capitalized** word to reveal five facts about the constellation of Sagittarius.

- Sagittarius is often depicted as a **TRUECAN**

- The figure's **ORRAW** is said to point at the heart of the Scorpius constellation

- In Greek mythology, the creature is occasionally interpreted as a satyr who invented **HEARCRY**

- In other interpretations, he helped the hero Jason in his quest for the golden **ELFCEE**

- Ancient Babylonians depicted the constellation as having two heads: one human, and one **HENTRAP**

Join the stars in order to reveal a picture of Sagittarius.

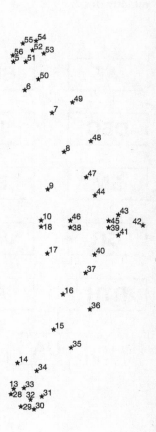

Rearrange these boxes to spell out seven words, all associated with Capricorn. Each box will be used exactly once.

AT	BER	CAR
DEC	DI	EA
EM	EY	GO
GR	JAN	NAL
RTH	RY	SAT
UA	URN	

Place the capitalized surnames of these Capricorn celebrities into the grid once each, crossword style.

3 letters
Muhammad ALI

4 letters
Nicolas CAGE
(LL) COOL (J)

5 letters
Orlando BLOOM
David BOWIE

Michelle OBAMA
Betty WHITE

6 letters
Jim CARREY
Bradley COOPER
Calvin HARRIS
Diane KEATON
John LEGEND
Ricky MARTIN

Dolly PARTON

7 letters
Lin-Manuel
　MIRANDA
Elvis PRESLEY

8 letters
Lewis HAMILTON

Reveal a word associated with those born under Capricorn by placing A, C, E, G, I, M, P, R or T into each empty square, so that no letter repeats in any row, column or bold-lined 3×3 box. Once solved, the word can be read down the shaded diagonal.

		I			G		R	
		G	A		C			I
	T							P
R				I			E	
	P			C				G
I							A	
C			P		R	E		
	M		T			P		

How many words can you find in this word square, including a nine-letter word that might describe a Capricorn? Make each word by starting on any letter square and then tracing a path to touching squares, including diagonally. Each word must be at least three letters in length, and a letter square can't be used more than once in a given word.

Targets:
Good: 25 words
Fantastic: 40 words

Can you find all the hidden stars in this grid? Clue numbers in some squares show the number of stars in touching squares – including diagonally. No more than one star can be placed per square, and there are no stars in the squares that contain numbers.

	3		2		2	
	5	3		3		1
	4				3	1
		4			4	
	1			4		3
2	3		3			
				1	1	1

Rearrange the letters within each column to reveal a quote about astrology, along with the person who it is attributed to. Words may be broken across lines, but every space is included no matter its position. Spaces are shown by empty boxes.

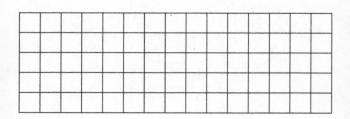

F	E	E	H	A	A	F	A	A	C	A	C	A	E	A
H	H	S	O	H	T	M	H	I	E	H	E	C	R	O
T	I	S	S	N	U	O	R	N	G	H	O	H	R	T
W	I			T		R	S.	R	I	I		T	T	T
	T				W				L		W			

How quickly can you navigate your way to the centre of this star map?

Crack the number-to-letter code by solving the following clues, writing each clue's answer in the squares beneath, with one letter per square. Once you have solved the code, reveal the Capricorn characteristic at the bottom of the page.

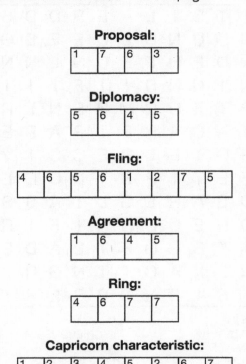

Proposal:

1	7	6	3

Diplomacy:

5	6	4	5

Fling:

4	6	5	6	1	2	7	5

Agreement:

1	6	4	5

Ring:

4	6	7	7

Capricorn characteristic:

1	2	3	4	5	2	6	7

Capricornians are known for a wide range of traits, including those listed below. Find them all in the word search, written in a straight line in any direction, including diagonally and backwards.

```
C I T S I L A E R D D S E
G R O U N D E D E E E G B
A N D P H F E D N L N N M
M N I N N S I I F I I I I
B P T Z U C M R S N L R S
I T A C A R E I P A P E C
T S O T E L R E C S I V H
I F E T I P B I D O C E I
O D E A R E G L I A S S E
U D N E U O N N I F I R V
S T T D L O E T L A D E O
Z N E X A C T I N G R P U
E L B I S N O P S E R T S
```

AMBITIOUS
DEDICATED
DETERMINED
DISCIPLINED
ENTERPRISING
EXACTING
FOCUSED
GROUNDED

LOGICAL
MISCHIEVOUS
PATIENT
PERSEVERING
REALISTIC
RESPONSIBLE
SELF-RELIANT
TRAILBLAZING

Can you crack the letter-shift code to reveal the names of three stars found in the constellation of Capricorn?

Just as the light from distant stars shifts in colour as it travels to earth, so each letter has been shifted by a fixed amount. For example, A might have become B; B might have become C, and so on, wrapping around from Z back to A.

Zmetudm

Eotqppu

Bmltmz

A	B	C	D	E	F	G	H	I	J	K	L	M

N	O	P	Q	R	S	T	U	V	W	X	Y	Z

Rearrange the order of the letters in each **capitalized** word to reveal five facts about the constellation of Capricorn.

- Capricorn depicts a hybrid creature, part **TOGA** and part fish

- One of the creature's horns is said to have been made into the cornucopia, the horn of **NETPLY**

- In other Greek myths, Capricorn represents the Greek god Pan – who escaped a monster by jumping into the **LINE**

- Capricorn is associated with the winter **ICESSLOT**

- The figure may also be connected to the Sumerian god of **SWIMDO**

Join the stars in order to reveal a picture of Capricorn.

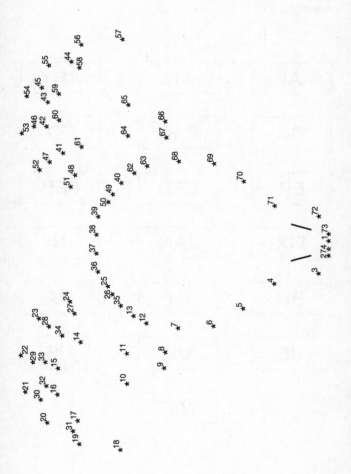

Rearrange these boxes to spell out seven words, all associated with Aquarius. Each box will be used exactly once.

AI	AN	ARY
BL	EAR	ED
ER	ERB	FEB
FIX	JAN	R
RU	RY	UA
UE	UR	US
	WAT	

Place the capitalized surnames of these Aquarius celebrities into the grid once each, crossword style.

3 letters
Dr DRE

4 letters
Chris ROCK
Elijah WOOD

6 letters
Isla FISHER
Michael JORDAN
Harry STYLES

7 letters
Jennifer ANISTON
Ashton KUTCHER
Kelly ROWLAND
Tom SELLECK

Ed SHEERAN
Oprah WINFREY

10 letters
Tom HIDDLESTON
Kerry WASHINGTON

Reveal a word associated with those born under Aquarius by placing A, D, E, I, L, N, S, T or V into each empty square, so that no letter repeats in any row, column or bold-lined 3×3 box. Once solved, the word can be read down the shaded diagonal.

			D			V		
D		A		T				
			E			L	N	
	S							
	L	T	V		I	D	A	
							E	
	A	S		V				
				L		S		N
		D			S			

How many words can you find in this word square, including a nine-letter word that might describe an Aquarius? Make each word by starting on any letter square and then tracing a path to touching squares, including diagonally. Each word must be at least three letters in length, and a letter square can't be used more than once in a given word.

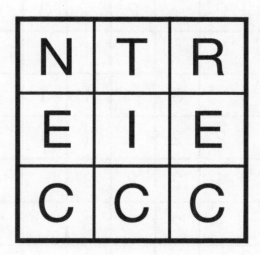

Targets:
Good: 15 words
Fantastic: 20 words

Can you find all the hidden stars in this grid? Clue numbers in some squares show the number of stars in touching squares – including diagonally. No more than one star can be placed per square, and there are no stars in the squares that contain numbers.

	2		2		3	
2				1		
1		3		1	1	
	2	2		1	1	1
	1	2	2	3		
2		2		3		2
	2		3		2	

Rearrange the letters within each column to reveal a quote about astrology, along with the person who it is attributed to. Words may be broken across lines, but every space is included no matter its position. Spaces are shown by empty boxes.

A	D	E	A	R	H	A	H	E	A
M	H	E	E	R	I	C	I	I	A
N	R	E.	E	S	K	E	L	L	E
R	S	H		T	S	L	R	O	F
T	T	H		W	T	N		S	L
		M			U	S		V	

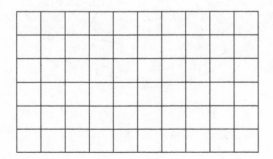

How quickly can you navigate your way to the centre of this star map?

Crack the number-to-letter code by solving the following clues, writing each clue's answer in the squares beneath, with one letter per square. Once you have solved the code, reveal the Aquarius characteristic at the bottom of the page.

Imitate:

5	6	5	6	1

Stylish:

1	2	6	1

Aquarius sign:

3	6	4

Getting dressed:

1	2	3	7	8	6	7	8

Sorcerer:

5	3	8	6	1	6	3	7

Aquarius characteristic:

1	2	3	4	5	6	7	8

Aquarians are known for a wide range of traits, including those listed below. Find them all in the word search, written in a straight line in any direction, including diagonally and backwards.

```
U F R E E S P I R I T E D S
T N X L N V I N C L I P E I
S A C A A N I E A N E L E N
I P I O C N R T D I F U X T
N F O P N E O I A S P O H R
N E V N B V V I U E D O L I
O E S R T I E F T O R A T G
V E A O D A F N H P N C U U
A L D U T I N T T O E N E I
T U A I C E R E I I I C N N
I L S I R O R T O Q O R X G
V I E I N E A I U U O N T E
E N E U N R C E C Q S E A R
T N A I R A T I N A M U H L
```

CEREBRAL
CREATIVE
ESOTERIC
EXCEPTIONAL
FREE-SPIRITED
HUMANITARIAN
INDIVIDUAL
INNOVATIVE

INTRIGUING
RATIONAL
SELF-SUFFICIENT
SPONTANEOUS
UNCONVENTIONAL
UNIQUE
UNORTHODOX
UTOPIAN

Can you crack the letter-shift code to reveal the names of three stars found in the constellation of Aquarius?

Just as the light from distant stars shifts in colour as it travels to earth, so each letter has been shifted by a fixed amount. For example, A might have become B; B might have become C, and so on, wrapping around from Z back to A.

Ygjgryaaj

Ygjgrskroq

Yqgz

A	B	C	D	E	F	G	H	I	J	K	L	M

N	O	P	Q	R	S	T	U	V	W	X	Y	Z

Rearrange the order of the letters in each **capitalized** word to reveal five facts about the constellation of Aquarius.

- The constellation is associated with the **LOGOFIND** of the Nile in Ancient Egypt

- In Babylonian mythology, the stars represent the god Ea and his water **SAVE**

- Greek mythology depicts the constellation as Ganymede, Zeus's cup **EREBAR**

- In some versions of the story, Ganymede is stolen by Zeus from Eos, goddess of the **WAND**

- In the Hindu zodiac, the constellation's name translates to 'water **RICHPET**'

Join the stars in order to reveal a picture of Aquarius.

Rearrange these boxes to spell out seven words, all associated with Pisces. Each box will be used exactly once.

EN	FEB	FI
GRE	LE	MA
MU	NE	NEP
RCH	RUA	RY
SH	TAB	TER

TU	WA

Place the capitalized names of these Pisces celebrities into the grid once each, crossword style.

4 letters
Jon Bon JOVI

5 letters
Simone BILES
Glenn CLOSE
Daniel CRAIG
Kristin DAVIS

6 letters
Justin BIEBER
Bruce WILLIS
Rebel WILSON

7 letters
Queen LATIFAH
RIHANNA
Olivia RODRIGO

8 letters
Bryan CRANSTON
Eva LONGORIA
Liza MINNELLI

9 letters
Drew BARRYMORE

Reveal a word associated with those born under Pisces by placing A, E, F, H, I, L, N, S or U into each empty square, so that no letter repeats in any row, column or bold-lined 3×3 box. Once solved, the word can be read down the shaded diagonal.

		I						N
			A	I	U			F
L							E	I
				U	S			
	E		N		I		U	
			H	A				
S	U							E
H			I	N	A			
A					L			

How many words can you find in this word square, including a nine-letter word that might describe a Pisces? Make each word by starting on any letter square and then tracing a path to touching squares, including diagonally. Each word must be at least three letters in length, and a letter square can't be used more than once in a given word.

Targets:
Good: 10 words
Fantastic: 20 words

Can you find all the hidden stars in this grid? Clue numbers in some squares show the number of stars in touching squares – including diagonally. No more than one star can be placed per square, and there are no stars in the squares that contain numbers.

1		3		3		1
2		4		4		2
	4		3		2	
		4				2
4			3			
3				2	4	
2			3			1

Rearrange the letters within each column to reveal a quote about astrology, along with the person who it is attributed to. Words may be broken across lines, but every space is included no matter its position. Spaces are shown by empty boxes.

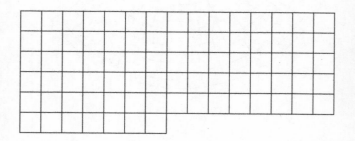

H	A	A	C	E	N	D	G	E	B	D	L	A	C	A
N	D	C	C	I	R	E	I	M	E	D	S	A	C	D
N	E	U	I	I	S	S	S	M	G	L	Y	.	S	D	O
W	E	V	I	L	S	S	Y	N	N	N			N	O
	F		V	O	U			O	O	O				T
	N		W	T										

How quickly can you navigate your way to the centre of this star map?

Crack the number-to-letter code by solving the following clues, writing each clue's answer in the squares beneath, with one letter per square. Once you have solved the code, reveal the Pisces characteristic at the bottom of the page.

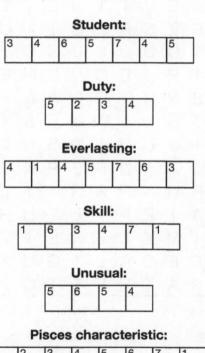

Student:

3	4	6	5	7	4	5

Duty:

5	2	3	4

Everlasting:

4	1	4	5	7	6	3

Skill:

1	6	3	4	7	1

Unusual:

5	6	5	4

Pisces characteristic:

1	2	3	4	5	6	7	1

Pisceans are known for a wide range of traits, including those listed below. Find them all in the word search, written in a straight line in any direction, including diagonally and backwards.

```
L T A E V I T N E T T A I
U A R E S P E C T F U L N
F C T U U U E E S C I A E
T C I P S E O U E M E V D
H E S N R T O R A S I E E
G P T S L I W G E S I G L
U T I C C U I O S N E W P
O I C A A N F E R N E P I
H N R U A R R H T T L G C
T G A T E P I L T U H I N
W U I M X L E N E I E Y I
G V E E O A L I G U A A R
E M P A T H E T I C P F P
```

ACCEPTING	GENTLE
ARTISTIC	GRACIOUS
ATTENTIVE	IMAGINATIVE
CARING	PRINCIPLED
EMPATHETIC	RESPECTFUL
EXPRESSIVE	THOUGHTFUL
FAITHFUL	TRUSTWORTHY
GENEROUS	WISE

Can you crack the letter-shift code to reveal the names of three stars found in the constellation of Pisces?

Just as the light from distant stars shifts in colour as it travels to earth, so each letter has been shifted by a fixed amount. For example, A might have become B; B might have become C, and so on, wrapping around from Z back to A.

Lwaspcr

Dtxxls

Ezcnfwlc

A	B	C	D	E	F	G	H	I	J	K	L	M

N	O	P	Q	R	S	T	U	V	W	X	Y	Z

Rearrange the order of the letters in each **capitalized** word to reveal five facts about the constellation of Pisces.

- Babylonian astrologers interpreted Pisces as two different figures: a **SLOWLAW**, and the 'Lady of **VANEHE**'

- The two fish are said to be the embodiment of **HOTPAIRED**, the Greek goddess of love, and her son **ROSE**

- In another tale, the fish **ENDDUG** the egg from which the goddess hatched onto the shore

- The two fish are said to have granted wishes to a man and his wife in **MERANG** folklore

- In Chinese astronomy, the constellation represents a **CEFNE** for containing a pig

Join the stars in order to reveal a picture of Pisces.

SOLUTION 1
- April
- Cardinal
- Fire
- March
- Mars
- Ram
- Red

SOLUTION 2

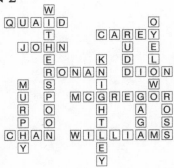

SOLUTION 3

SOLUTION 4
Words to find include **ambitious**, atom, bit, bits, bus, bust, but, buts, iota, its, mat, mats, moat,

moats, omit, omits, oust, out, outs, stub, sub, submit, suit, tam, tom, tomb, tombs, tub and tubs

SOLUTION 5

●		1	2	●	2	●
2	3	●		2		2
●		2	●	2	2	●
3	3				●	2
●	●	3	3	3		1
●	5	●	●	●	2	
2	●	3		3	●	1

SOLUTION 6

A		P	H	Y	S	I	C	I	A	N		W	I	T
H	O	U	T		A		K	N	O	W	L	E	D	G
E		O	F		A	S	T	R	O	L	O	G	Y	
H	A	S		N	O		R	I	G	H	T		T	O
	C	A	L	L		H	I	M	S	E	L	F		A
	P	H	Y	S	I	C	I	A	N.		H	I	P	P
O	C	R	A	T	E	S								

"A physician without a knowledge of Astrology has no right to call himself a physician." – Hippocrates

SOLUTION 7

SOLUTION 8

- Aim
- Mad
- Manic

- Day
- May
- Dynamic

SOLUTION 9

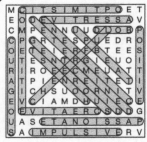

SOLUTION 10

Shift each letter back by 4 to reveal:

- Hamal
- Sheratan

- Mesarthim

SOLUTION 11

- The name 'Aries' comes from the Latin word for RAM
- The constellation was once believed to depict a FARMHAND
- In Greek mythology, Aries RESCUED the children of King Athamas

- Before becoming a constellation, Aries had a famous GOLDEN fleece
- Aries has sometimes been depicted with WINGS

SOLUTION 12

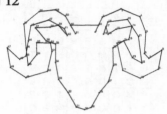

SOLUTION 13
- April
- Bull
- Earth
- Fixed
- Green
- May
- Venus

SOLUTION 14

SOLUTION 15

C	E	S	O	T	D	R	M	I
D	O	R	I	C	M	E	T	S
I	T	M	S	E	R	D	O	C
R	D	E	M	O	C	S	I	T
O	S	T	R	I	E	C	D	M
M	C	I	D	S	T	O	R	E
S	M	O	E	D	I	T	C	R
T	I	D	C	R	S	M	E	O
E	R	C	T	M	O	I	S	D

SOLUTION 16

Words to find include ace, aced, acid, aid, aide, aided, ate, cat, cede, ceded, cite, cited, decide, decided, dedicate, **dedicated**, dice, diced, did, die, diet, eat, eddied, edit, edited, eta, ice, iced, idea, tea, tide, tided, tie and tied

SOLUTION 17

1			1	2	●	1
●	1	1	●	3	3	
2	2	2		3	●	●
2	●			●	4	3
2	●	●	5	3		●
	4	●	●	●	4	2
●		2	4	●	3	●

SOLUTION 18

A	S	T	R	O	L	O	G	Y	
R	E	V	E	A	L	S		T	H
E		W	I	L	L		O	F	
T	H	E		G	O	D	S.		J
U	V	E	N	A	L				

"Astrology reveals the will of the gods." – Juvenal

SOLUTION 19

SOLUTION 20
- Adore
- Earn
- Hero
- Code
- Care
- Anchored

SOLUTION 21

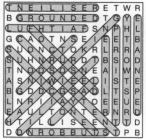

SOLUTION 22
Shift each letter back by 2 to reveal:
- Aldebaran
- Hyades
- Pleiades

SOLUTION 23

- Taurus may have been depicted as a bull in early CAVE paintings
- The constellation features a star cluster known as the Seven SISTERS
- Ancient Egyptians saw Taurus as a sign of new life in SPRING
- In Greek mythology, Taurus may represent the Cretan bull which created the MINOTAUR
- In Inuit mythology, the constellation contains a star which represents a hunted POLAR bear

SOLUTION 24

SOLUTION 25

- Air
- June
- May
- Mercury
- Mutable
- Twins
- Yellow

SOLUTION 26

SOLUTION 27

S	C	T	E	N	I	R	D	V
R	E	I	V	D	C	N	S	T
V	D	N	T	R	S	E	C	I
C	I	E	S	V	D	T	R	N
D	T	R	C	I	N	V	E	S
N	S	V	R	E	T	C	I	D
E	R	S	D	T	V	I	N	C
T	N	C	I	S	E	D	V	R
I	V	D	N	C	R	S	T	E

SOLUTION 28

Words to find include aerie, ail, air, airs, are, ares, art, ear, earl, ears, eat, eel, era, eras, erase, ere, eve, ever, eves, ire, ires, lee, leer, leers, lees, lei, lever, levers, liar, liars, lie, lira, lire, lit, litre, litres, rail, rat, reel, rev, revel, rile, sail, sari, sat, satire, sea, sear, seat, see, seer, sere, serve, sever, tail, tar, tare, tares, tars, tie, tier, tiers, tile, tire, tires, trail, tree, trees, veer, veers, veil, **versatile** and verse

SOLUTION 29

1	2			2	4	●
1	●	●	4	●	●	●
	3	●	●	3		3
	2	3		2	2	●
1	●			●	3	2
2		2		2	3	●
●	2	●	2	●	2	1

SOLUTION 30

W E		A R E		M E R E L Y		T
H E		S T A R S'		T E N N I S
	B A L L S,		S T R U C K		A
N D		B A N D E D		W H I C H
	W A Y		P L E A S E		T H E
M.		J O H N		W E B S T E R	

"We are merely the stars' tennis balls, struck and banded which way please them." – John Webster

SOLUTION 31

SOLUTION 32
- Zeus
- Sea
- Soul
- Use
- Sole
- Zealous

SOLUTION 33

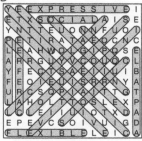

SOLUTION 34
Shift each letter back by 8 to reveal:
- Pollux
- Castor
- Alhena

SOLUTION 35
- The stars Castor and Pollux are referred to in Babylonian mythology as the Great TWINS
- They were both said to be depictions of the Babylonian god of the UNDERWORLD
- In Greek mythology, Pollux asked that his brother be made IMMORTAL, so Zeus turned them into stars
- The pair are considered to be the protectors of SAILORS
- They are often depicted riding HORSES

SOLUTION 36

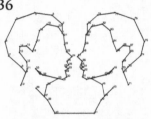

SOLUTION 37
- Cardinal
- Crab
- July
- June
- Moon
- Silver
- Water

SOLUTION 38

```
  F     H
  O     A            OH     W
G R A N D E          F      H
  D     K            F      I
B       S T R E E P  R      T
A                    R      A
C R U I S E    M U S K      K
O          T         A      E
N     K A L I N G    R      R
           R
      V E R G A R A
```

SOLUTION 39

N	G	A	S	T	U	R	I	D
S	U	T	R	D	I	N	G	A
D	I	R	A	G	N	S	U	T
R	S	U	T	I	G	D	A	N
A	N	G	D	U	S	T	R	I
I	T	D	N	A	R	G	S	U
G	D	N	U	S	A	I	T	R
T	A	I	G	R	D	U	N	S
U	R	S	I	N	T	A	D	G

SOLUTION 40

Words to find include ant, ante, anti, ate, **attentive**, eta, native, nee, net, nit, tan, tat, tee, teen, ten, tent, tie, tin, tine, tint, tit, titan, vein, vent, vet, vie and vine

SOLUTION 41

●	1		2	●	2	1
2		1	●	2	2	●
●			3		4	3
2	2	3	●	●	●	●
1	●		●	5	●	3
	3	3		3	3	
●	2	●	2	●	2	●

SOLUTION 42

I		H	A	V	E		L	O	V	E	D
T	H	E		S	T	A	R	S		T	O	O
	F	O	N	D	L	Y		T	O		B	E
	F	E	A	R	F	U	L		O	F		T
H	E		N	I	G	H	T	.		S	A	R	A
H		W	I	L	L	I	A	M	S

"I have loved the stars too fondly to be fearful of the night." – Sarah Williams

SOLUTION 43

SOLUTION 44
- Nice
- Magic
- Gem
- Imagine
- Magnetic
- Enigmatic

SOLUTION 45

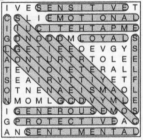

SOLUTION 46
Shift each letter back by 3 to reveal:
- Tarf
- Acubens
- Tegmine

SOLUTION 47

- The constellation of Cancer was recorded by the ASTRONOMER Ptolemy, though he gave it the Greek name Karkinos
- The giant crab Karkinos is supposed to have bitten the hero HERCULES during his twelve tasks
- The Greek goddess HERA placed the crab into the sky as a reward
- In Ancient Babylonia, the constellation may have been interpreted as a TURTLE
- Ancient Egyptians referred to the constellation as a SCARAB beetle

SOLUTION 48

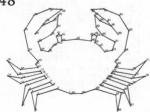

SOLUTION 49

- August
- Fire
- Fixed
- Gold
- July
- Lion
- Sun

SOLUTION 50

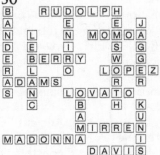

SOLUTION 51

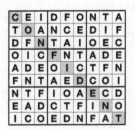

SOLUTION 52
Words to find include sac, sic, via, vicious, visa, viva, **vivacious** and vivas

SOLUTION 53

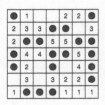

SOLUTION 54

I		W	I	L	L		L	O	O	K		O	N	
T	H	E		S	T	A	R	S		A	N	D		T
H	E	E	,		A	N	D		R	E	A	D		T	H
E		P	A	G	E		O	F		T	H	Y		D
E	S	T	I	N	Y	.		L	E	T	I	T	I	A
L	A	N	D	O	N									

"I will look on the stars and thee, and read the page of thy destiny." – Letitia Landon

SOLUTION 55

SOLUTION 56

- Flow
- Pure
- Fur
- Prowl
- Wolf
- Powerful

SOLUTION 57

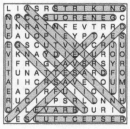

167

SOLUTION 58

Shift each letter back by 10 to reveal:
- Regulus
- Denebola
- Zosma

SOLUTION 59

- Leo's star, REGULUS, is one of the brightest in the night sky
- The lion is said to be the one killed in the FIRST of the twelve labours of a Greek hero
- According to the myth, the ferocious lion could not be harmed by any WEAPON
- In Ancient Sumer, the constellation was said to depict a MONSTER killed by Gilgamesh
- The constellation features a curved string of stars known as the SICKLE

SOLUTION 60

SOLUTION 61

- August
- Brown
- Earth
- Maiden
- Mercury
- Mutable
- September

SOLUTION 62

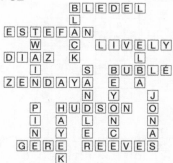

SOLUTION 63

SOLUTION 64

Words to find include age, aged, ago, anger, are, deign, drag, drain, ego, era, erg, ergo, gain, gin, gore, gored, grain, groan, nag, oar, oared, ogre, orange, ore, organ, **organized**, rag, rage, raged, rain, ran, rang, range, ranged, red, regain, reign, rein, roan, zero, zing, zinged and zinger

SOLUTION 65

	2	2	2	●		1
3	●	●			3	●
●	●	●		1	●	3
3	5	3		3	5	●
●			●	2	●	●
	3	3			3	5	●
1	●	2	●		1	2	●

SOLUTION 66

S	O		R	E	Q	U	I	S	I	T	E		I	S		T	H	E
	U	S	E		O	F		A	S	T	R	O	L	O	G	Y		T
O		T	H	E		A	R	T	S		O	F		D	I	V	I	N
A	T	I	O	N,		A	S		I	T		W	E	R	E		T	H
E		K	E	Y		T	H	A	T		O	P	E	N	S		T	H
E		D	O	O	R		O	F		A	L	L		T	H	E	I	R
	M	Y	S	T	E	R	I	E	S.		H	E	I	N	R	I	C	H
	C	O	R	N	E	L	I	U	S		A	G	R	I	P	P	A	

"So requisite is the use of Astrology to the Arts of Divination, as it were the Key that opens the door of all their Mysteries." – Heinrich Cornelius Agrippa

SOLUTION 67

SOLUTION 68
- True
- Result
- Rules
- Set
- Routes
- Resolute

SOLUTION 69

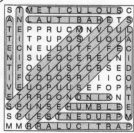

SOLUTION 70
Shift each letter back by 5 to reveal:
- Spica
- Porrima
- Heze

SOLUTION 71
- Virgo is the LARGEST constellation in the zodiac
- Some cultures have depicted Virgo as a maiden, holding a set of SCALES
- Virgo is associated with the goddess Persephone, who was kidnapped by HADES and taken to the Greek underworld
- The maiden Virgo is frequently associated with WHEAT
- Babylonian depictions of Virgo are interpreted as a goddess holding a PALM leaf

SOLUTION 72

SOLUTION 73
- Air
- Cardinal
- October
- Pink
- Scales
- September
- Venus

SOLUTION 74

SOLUTION 75

SOLUTION 76

Words to find include aegis, age, ages, are, ares, art, arts, ate, ates, cigar, cigars, ear, ears, eat, era, eta, gate, gates, gear, gears, get, gets, gist, ice, ices, rag, rage, rages, raise, rat, rate, rates, rest, sea, sear, seat, set, sic, **strategic**, tag, tar, tare, tares, tars, tart, tarts, tea, tear, tears, teat, test, tragic, tragics and treat

SOLUTION 77

●	1	1	1	2	●	1
2			●	3	2	2
●	1		2		●	1
1	1	1	2	●	2	
1	1		●	4		1
1	●		3	●	●	3
	2	●	2	3	●	●

SOLUTION 78

W	I	T	H	O	U	T		A	S	T	R	O	L	O
G	Y		M	A	N		T	R	E	A	D	S,		A
S		I	T		W	E	R	E,		I	N		T	H
E		D	I	M		T	W	I	L	I	G	H	T	
O	F		I	G	N	O	R	A	N	C	E.		L	U
K	E		D	E	N	N	I	S		B	R	O	U	G
H	T	O	N											

"Without astrology man treads, as it were, in the dim twilight of ignorance." – Luke Dennis Broughton

SOLUTION 79

SOLUTION 80

- Air
- Aurora
- Saga
- Curious
- Crisis
- Gracious

SOLUTION 81

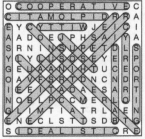

SOLUTION 82

Shift each letter back by 7 to reveal:

- Zubenelgenubi
- Zubeneschamali
- Brachium

SOLUTION 83
- The scales are associated with Astraea, the goddess of JUSTICE
- Several civilizations have characterized the scales as a pair of SCORPION claws
- The connection to balance may be linked to Libra's connection to the AUTUMNAL equinox
- Ancient Egyptians interpreted Libra's three brightest stars as forming the shape of a BOAT
- Libra is the only astrological sign whose symbol is an INANIMATE object

SOLUTION 84

SOLUTION 85
- Black
- Fixed
- November
- October
- Pluto
- Scorpion
- Water

SOLUTION 86

SOLUTION 87

SOLUTION 88

Words to find include ass, assert, **assertive**, asset, aver, avert, ease, eases, ere, reset, rev, revs, save, saver, saves, sea, seas, see, seer, sees, sere, seres, set, tea, teas, tease, teaser, teases, tee, tees, tie, tier, ties, tree, trees, tress, vase, vases, veer, vet, vie and vies

SOLUTION 89

1	●	1		1	2	●
2		3	2	●		2
	●	3	●		2	●
1	2	●	4		4	3
	2	4	●	●	●	●
2	●		●		5	4
●	2	2		2	●	●

SOLUTION 90

T	H	E		S	O	U	L		O	F		T	H	E		N	E
W	L	Y		B	O	R	N		B	A	B	Y		I	S		M
A	R	K	E	D		F	O	R		L	I	F	E		B	Y	
T	H	E		P	A	T	T	E	R	N		O	F		T	H	E
	S	T	A	R	S		A	T		T	H	E		M	O	M	E
N	T		I	T		C	O	M	E	S		I	N	T	O		T
H	E		W	O	R	L	D.		J	O	H	A	N	N	E	S	
K	E	P	L	E	R												

"The soul of the newly born baby is marked for life by the pattern of the stars at the moment it comes into the world." – Johannes Kepler

SOLUTION 91

SOLUTION 92
- Aims
- Boss
- Motto
- Utmost
- Boast
- Ambitious

SOLUTION 93

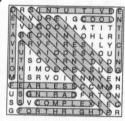

SOLUTION 94
Shift each letter back by 1 to reveal:
- Vespertilio
- Shaula
- Sargas

SOLUTION 95
- The Scorpian stars Shaula and Lesath both have names which mean STING
- In Greek mythology, the scorpion was sent to challenge the hunter ORION, and both were made into constellations
- The scorpion was supposedly sent by the hunter goddess ARTEMIS
- Some Hawaiians interpret the constellation as the FISH-HOOK of the demigod Maui
- In Javanese Indonesia, the constellation's name refers to its similarity to a COCONUT tree

SOLUTION 96

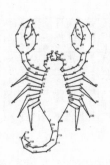

SOLUTION 97

- Archer
- December
- Fire
- Jupiter
- Mutable
- November
- Purple

SOLUTION 98

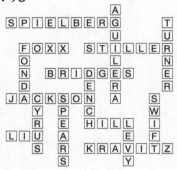

SOLUTION 99

T	V	C	E	I	K	L	A	O
O	A	E	T	C	L	K	I	V
K	I	L	O	V	A	E	C	T
I	T	A	K	L	V	O	E	C
V	L	O	C	A	E	T	K	I
C	E	K	I	O	T	V	L	A
A	K	T	V	E	C	I	O	L
E	C	I	L	T	O	A	V	K
L	O	V	A	K	I	C	T	E

SOLUTION 100

Words to find include able, adapt, **adaptable**, alb, ale, apt, ate, bale, bat, bleat, dale, data, date, eat, eta, lab, lad, lap, late, lea, lead, let, pad, pal, palate, pale, pat, pate, tab, table, tale, tap, tea and teal

SOLUTION 101

●	2	●	●	●	3	1
2	4	3	5	●	3	●
●		●	2	2		3
2	4	2			●	●
●						3
2	4	2		●	2	●
●	2	●		1	2	1

SOLUTION 102

T	H	E	R	E		I	S		N	O		B	E	T
T	E	R		B	O	A	T		T	H	A	N		A
	H	O	R	O	S	C	O	P	E		T	O		H
E	L	P		M	A	N		C	R	O	S	S		O
V	E	R		T	H	E		S	E	A		O	F	
L	I	F	E.		V	A	H	A	R	A	M	A	H	I
R	A													

"There is no better boat than a horoscope to help man cross over the sea of life." – Vaharamahira

SOLUTION 103

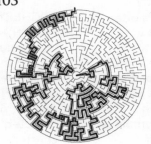

SOLUTION 104
- Fun
- Afar
- Aura
- Druid
- Fad
- Unafraid

SOLUTION 105

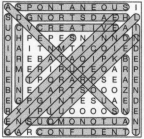

SOLUTION 106
Shift each letter back by 9 to reveal:
- Nunki
- Ascella
- Polis

SOLUTION 107

- Sagittarius is often depicted as a CENTAUR
- The figure's ARROW is said to point at the heart of the Scorpius constellation
- In Greek mythology, the creature is occasionally interpreted as a satyr who invented ARCHERY
- In other interpretations, he helped the hero Jason in his quest for the golden FLEECE
- Ancient Babylonians depicted the constellation as having two heads: one human, and one PANTHER

SOLUTION 108

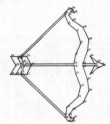

SOLUTION 109

- Cardinal
- December
- Earth
- Goat
- Grey
- January
- Saturn

SOLUTION 110

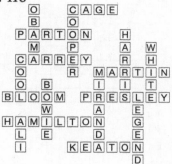

SOLUTION 111

SOLUTION 112

Words to find include act, active, actor, are, atop, aver, cap, car, care, carp, carve, cat, cave, coat, cop, copra, core, cot, ear, eat, era, oar, octave, ore, pact, par, pare, pat, pave, pore, pot, pro, **proactive**, rap, rat, rave, react, reap, rev, rot, taco, tap, tar, tare, taro, top, tor, tore, vat and via

SOLUTION 113

●	3	●	2	●	2	●
●	5	3		3		1
●	4	●	●	●	3	1
●		4	●	●	4	●
	1		●	4	●	3
2	3		3			●
●	●	●	●	1	1	1

SOLUTION 114

T	H	E		H	U	M	A	N		H	E	A	R	T
	I	S		A		F	R	A	I	L		C	R	A
F	T		O	N		W	H	I	C	H		W	E	
W	I	S	H		T	O		R	E	A	C	H		T
H	E		S	T	A	R	S	.		G	I	O	T	T	O

"The human heart is a frail craft on which we wish to reach the stars." – Giotto

SOLUTION 115

SOLUTION 116
- Plan
- Tact
- Catapult

- Pact
- Call
- Punctual

SOLUTION 117

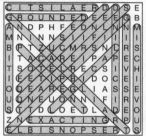

SOLUTION 118

Shift each letter back by 12 to reveal:

- Nashira
- Scheddi
- Pazhan

SOLUTION 119

- Capricorn depicts a hybrid creature, part GOAT and part fish
- One of the creature's horns is said to have been made into the cornucopia, the horn of PLENTY
- In other Greek myths, Capricorn represents the Greek god Pan – who escaped a monster by jumping into the NILE
- Capricorn is associated with the winter SOLSTICE
- The figure may also be connected to the Sumerian god of WISDOM

SOLUTION 120

SOLUTION 121

- Air
- Blue
- February
- Fixed
- January
- Uranus
- Water-bearer

SOLUTION 122

SOLUTION 123

I	E	L	D	S	N	V	T	A
D	N	A	L	T	V	E	S	I
S	T	V	I	E	A	L	N	D
A	S	N	E	D	L	T	I	V
E	L	T	V	N	I	D	A	S
V	D	I	S	A	T	N	E	L
L	A	S	N	V	E	I	D	T
T	I	E	A	L	D	S	V	N
N	V	D	T	I	S	A	L	E

SOLUTION 124

Words to find include cent, centre, cite, **eccentric**, enter, entice, entire, ice, inter, ire, net, nice, nicer, niece, nit, nitre, recent, recite, rein, rice, rite, ten, tie, tier, tin, tine, tire and trice

SOLUTION 125

●	2		2	●	3	●
2		●		1		●
1	●	3		1	1	
	2	2	●	1	1	1
●	1	2	2	3		●
2		2	●	3	●	2
●	2	●	3	●	2	

SOLUTION 126

T	H	E		S	T	A	R	S
A	R	E		T	H	E		L	A
N	D	M	A	R	K	S		O	F
	T	H	E		U	N	I	V	E
R	S	E	.		W	I	L	L	I	A
M		H	E	R	S	C	H	E	L

"The stars are the landmarks of the universe."
– William Herschel

SOLUTION 127

SOLUTION 128

- Mimic
- Chic
- Air
- Changing
- Magician
- Charming

SOLUTION 129

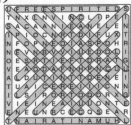

SOLUTION 130

Shift each letter back by 6 to reveal:

- Sadalsuud
- Sadalmelik
- Skat

SOLUTION 131

- The constellation is associated with the FLOODING of the Nile in Ancient Egypt
- In Babylonian mythology, the stars represent the god Ea and his water VASE
- Greek mythology depicts the constellation as Ganymede, Zeus's cup BEARER
- In some versions of the story, Ganymede is stolen by Zeus from Eos, goddess of the DAWN
- In the Hindu zodiac, the constellation's name translates to 'water PITCHER'

SOLUTION 132

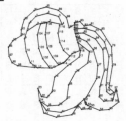

SOLUTION 133

- February
- Fish
- Green
- March
- Mutable
- Neptune
- Water

SOLUTION 134

```
        B   RODRIGO
  J  I     I
  O  L  H     BIEBER
  V  E  A           A
WILSON              R
  I  A     N  M     R
  L  T  DAVIS  I    Y
  L  I        N    M
  I  F  CRANSTON
  S  A     R  E
     H  A  CLOSE
        I     L
  LONGORIA
```

SOLUTION 135

U	F	I	S	E	L	A	H	N
E	N	H	A	I	U	S	L	F
L	A	S	F	H	N	U	E	I
I	H	L	E	U	S	N	F	A
F	E	A	N	L	I	H	U	S
N	S	U	H	A	F	E	I	L
S	U	N	L	F	H	I	A	E
H	L	E	I	N	A	F	S	U
A	I	F	U	S	E	L	N	H

SOLUTION 136

Words to find include air, airs, airy, arson, ion, nary, noisy, oar, oars, rain, ran, sin, sir, soar, son, sonar, vain, van, vary, via, vision and **visionary**

SOLUTION 137

1	●	3	●	3	●	1
2		4	●	4		2
●	4	●	3	●	2	●
●	●	4				2
4	●	●	3	●		●
3	●	●		2	4	●
2	●	●	3	●		1

SOLUTION 138

H	E	A	V	E	N		S	E	N	D	S		D	O
W	N		I	T	S		G	O	O	D		A	N	D
	E	V	I	L		S	Y	M	B	O	L	S		A
N	D		W	I	S	E		M	E	N		A	C	T
	A	C	C	O	R	D	I	N	G	L	Y	.		C	O
N	F	U	C	I	U	S								

"Heaven sends down its good and evil symbols and wise men act accordingly." – Confucius

SOLUTION 139

SOLUTION 140
- Learner
- Role
- Eternal

- Talent
- Rare
- Tolerant

SOLUTION 141

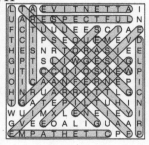

SOLUTION 142
Shift each letter back by 11 to reveal:
- Alpherg
- Simmah
- Torcular

SOLUTION 143

- Babylonian astrologers interpreted Pisces as two different figures: a SWALLOW, and the 'Lady of HEAVEN'
- The two fish are said to be the embodiment of APHRODITE, the Greek goddess of love, and her son EROS
- In another tale, the fish NUDGED the egg from which the goddess hatched onto the shore
- The two fish are said to have granted wishes to a man and his wife in GERMAN folklore
- In Chinese astronomy, the constellation represents a FENCE for containing a pig

SOLUTION 144